This Small Book is dedicated to Mollie Cameron-Young

My mother's Sister, Who taught me that Animals are

People

Adult Franklin Gull

Form, Beauty,Aerodynamic Purity, and Function .

THIS IS MY STORY

An account, with some embroidery, of life sharing

A residence and time period with a Human Person

From a Bird Person's perspective

Written by   Frankie   and Michael A Pope

ILLUSTRATIONS

Franklin Gull in flight - Page 2 Jack Vincent

Cover and back - Greg Lavaty

Scot Hein--heinphoto.com

Other illustrations are from the Author's files

Line Drawings Courtesy of U.S. Fish and Wildlife

My thanks to my many friends who encouraged me and

particularly to Ma. Daphne D. Piamonte and Jennifer

McVaugh who read and re read the text for me, offering

many valuable suggestions.

CONTENTS:

Copyright Page   listed as- My name is Frankie

This is my story.

An account of living with a crippled   Gull

I shared some five months with a crippled Franklin's Gull   I discovered that this bird was remarkably intelligent, and made a fine companion. I feel that this was a unique experience that I want to share with others. I tried writing a type of diary or narrative diary and found it deadly dull. I doubted if even avid bird watchers would benefit much from it. I hope that approaching it from the Bird People's point of view has made it more interesting.

These particular birds fly over vast distances and cope with differing climates, yet their survival rate is remarkable.I think we have a lot to learn from our Feathered Friends.

CHAPTER I, Drowning.

The Scene, a small coastal village in Western Mexico.

Louisa awoke to the call of the Rooster who lived just down the road; the old one that had a crack in his voice.

It was the first grey light of dawn.

Today the sea was much quieter. Some days in the last week you could feel the ground shake when a big wave broke on the beach. To Louise the Sea sounded angry.

Today the water almost whispered with just an occasional crack and boom.

She lay there luxuriating in the soft warmth of early morning. Enjoying the sensations of being snug in her sleeping bag and yet still be virtually out doors so close to the ocean.

She felt secure in her large empty tent next to the converted bus. There were mesh windows on all sides so she could survey the village on one side and the beach on the other. She stirred herself, what a fine time for a beach walk.

The only clothing in the tent was her evening dress from the dinner the previous night. She had showered and dressed in the bus before going out for dinner with her daughter Elisa and Doby her perhaps too handsome young man. Louisa came from an age where couples were married. She liked Doby for his relaxed easy going ways and impeccable manners but had to stop herself from referring to him as Elisa's husband. That apparently was not cool. When they had all came home tired and full of good fish and wine they had separated.

Louisa did not want to intrude on the young people at this hour to rummage through her suitcase for shorts and a top. Besides, "Why can't I wear any thing I like, there will be no one on the beach at this hour". So she slipped on her "Little Black Dress" and crawled out of her tent.

She walked on the high built up sand close to the palms for the kilometer or so to the north end of the beach. Sat on the rocks for a while looking out to sea past the headland. She thought "I must look like one of those disjointed modern paintings. A small shoeless woman with tousled short blond hair sitting on a rock at the end of a deserted Mexican beach dressed only in stylish skimpy black cocktail dress. Pity there is no one to paint me".

She picked her way back along the waters edge, as the first rays of the sun started to peek over the low hills behind the beach.

As she walked along she noticed an object being washed back and forth in the white water and foam rolled over by succeeding waves. She had to get quite close before she recognized it as a bird.

It only moved once in a while and was trailing one wing in the foam as the waves swept by.

The bird had its beak open and was gasping for air. With no further thought Louisa rushed into the waves. Up to her waist at times, she caught the creature and carried it up the beach. It was soaked through, the water proofing gone from most of its feathers, bedraggled and covered in sand.

The Gull had a red tinted tip to its beak and a cute black head with a white eyeliner.

Louisa later said that the bird had such an intelligent look.

For Louisa it was love at first sight. She looked the bird over and there was no other obvious damage apart from the broken wing. Louisa cooed and spoke to it in French baby talk. The bird was past caring. Wrapping it in the abbreviated hem of her dress Elisa hurried back to the bus.

CHAPTER 11 Adopted

Hi I'm Frankie. I am a seagull. Not just any seagull but a female member of a particular tribe. We are called Franklin's Gulls. We were named after John Franklin, an English Navy chap who discovered the Northwest Passage. He died in the frozen Arctic a hundred and sixty years ago.

You, human people, think you are the only smart tribe around. I suppose that it is just because you build airplanes and computers and stuff. Well, you know not everyone needs all those aids. We Franklins don't need planes. We fly really well without them. We don't need computers either; we can navigate just fine without GPS. We know where we are, and usually what the weather is going to be like tomorrow.   I know there is no listing on Dow Jones that will tell you where to find juicy bugs next month so who needs all that?

You know!   Perhaps the reason that some people go around calling others "Bird Brain" is that they feel a little inferior. They secretly know the birds are smart; after all they are always looking up to us. Poor people ------it must be a problem.

We birds are smart in different ways that humans do not know about yet, but we still make mistakes and I had made a big one! So I ended up in the surf slowly drowning.

My wing was broken. One foot and claws were tangled in the feathers of the broken wing. I could not swim or paddle. I could not walk. I could not fly. I was done for!

When I saw this sort of white headed black creature rushing towards me I did not recognize it as a human. I mean, I do not hang out with humans who wear "Little Black Dresses". I thought it was some type of predator that was strange to me. I only wondered how my life was going to end. Is it going to bite me, or chew on me, swallow me whole or what?

The creature picked me up gently; I was really at a loss. It's a human female! Do they eat gulls?

Oh no, she's speaking French! I've heard what they do with snails and frogs, oh horror; I hear the French will eat anything.

Goodbye life, it was fun!

You never know what is next do you? Here I thought for a moment that I was going to slip right in there on the menu between the "Pate de foi grass" and the "Entrée" and this woman is busy falling in love with me.

I have never been this close to a human before.

I am certainly not feeling my best; in fact, I am near dead.

But still, I have to say you human guys have problems.   These long gangly things they call fingers; All warm and a little greasy and pokey.   They don't smell of any thing good like fish or grasshoppers. Still you know, that smell that humans have hangs in there, it just sticks to you.

It became apparent that she was not going to eat me. Well, at least not right away.

I relaxed a lot. I did not have much choice.

I was just about dead, so full of sand and sea that I could not have flown even if I had four good wings.

You know humans, now I know you a bit better, I will tell you:

If you want to pick up a bird and make it feel better don't do it with those stinky pokey fingers. Get a nice clean towel or something, That way we birds don't feel that we need a shower right away when you let us go. It is so much more civilized. I know you mean well, but just think of being handled by a big slimy snake and you will get the message.

Sorry, that sounds rude; I got sort of carried away there.

It's just that some smells seem to just really stick to you. You know like garlic or onions or some "too old" fish. Now, if all humans smelled like fresh sardines I would not worry a bit.

It is not only that. Sometimes you guys have stuff on your hands like detergent or petroleum that upsets the oil our body puts on our feathers. It's a big,

every day job, looking after three thousand feathers. One does not need anything that will make the job any longer!

This lady, and she was a lady (you can tell by the smell, they wear that expensive subtle perfume) had apparently decided to adopt me.

If I had to choose a new mother I could have done a lot worse. She was not very big as humans go, not too tall, and not too old, but well, sort of mature, friendly looking and kind of cute. I mean she wasn't really beautiful like my own mother –but, for a human, pretty good!

Any way my new mum cradled me in her arms and wrapped a bit of her dress around me and started talking to me in French. I was glad I had learned a little of the language from the farmhands who worked close to our nesting area in Canada.

We, my new mum and I, walked a long way down the beach to a big old school bus, which was painted green, with a tent beside it.

Louisa (my new mum's name)   was visiting from France for a month. Her daughter, Elisa lived with a French tattooed guy called Doby (who smelled a bit of garlic) in his artistically converted bus. Elisa told her mum that he was very clever with his hands. I did not understand why they both giggled at that.

For the next three weeks I was all but loved to death. They made me a little nest in a box, with my own blanket.

I spent most of my time wrapped in a towel on Louisa's lap, cooed over and talked to, in at least three different languages. Treated like a queen. Well it was easier than catching fish and bugs for a living.

My new family consisted of Louisa, her daughter Elisa, her (hopefully, in the future, son in law) Doby, and a large cat.

My life wrapped in a towel on Louisa's lap was really quite pleasant, a bit too much petting and stroking but I could tell she meant well. I felt quite safe and secure.

What a shock though after I was put down in my box. This huge cat's head appeared over the edge of the box. My heart stopped beating for a moment, then, it slowly and irregularly came back to life.

The cat was not snarling. Its mouth was closed. It was only sniffing and looking me over. Maybe they have fed the beast already? god I hope so!

The head disappeared. I was expecting the horrible thing to leap on me and maul and cripple me before playing with my broken body for an hour or two like I had seen other cats do with mice.

When I felt brave enough I stretched my neck way up to peek over the edge of the box and "THERE" was its   fat   butt   strolling slowly away. -----------------Phew!   I   said. Guess that ,as I was Louisa's Pet ,and Louisa was cool, so it was O.K. by him, he would not eat me.

Maybe the dumb animal thought all French women came equipped with a seagull . Que Sera Sera!

I had an unfortunate experience with the Daughter. I slept a lot the first week I was there.

One time when I was sleeping she thought I had died and stuck her head down very close to me to check. I woke up with a start and instinctively pecked her on the face. Well you should have heard the carry on. I guess I scared her but really I had not tried to peck her eye out. I had just tried to protect myself from the soup pot.

Up to that point I think she liked me but after that "La Concorde est Fini"!

The food was not great. They fed me all sorts of scraps mostly fishy stuff that was not really fresh.

I guess they though I was like those other gulls, the big ones that eat garbage.

I just could not make them understand that I needed good high vitamin organic bugs that wriggled.

My real mother always said. "If it isn't wriggling don't eat it. It isn't fresh."

They made me a little run out of chicken wire. I could stand up now but could not walk much, as I kept tripping on my broken wing which just dragged on the ground. I would accidentally step on it.

29

I would get frustrated; patience was never one of my long suits, My claws or toenails would get all tangled in my wing. I would fall down and I would cry from the pain.

Then someone would have to come and sort me out. I would get all stinky again from the fingers. It was not great.

The day was approaching when Louisa had to go back to France. What can we do with the Bird? This was discussed at great length.

Well if the daughter had her way it was Sea Gull Soup, with garlic, any day soon.

Young Garlic breath smoked another cigarette (funny smelling Tobacco) and tried to convince himself

that they could just let me go and I would survive? -----
For a while ---but that's nature.   My new mother was
not very happy.

She is a romantic, she believes love conquers all. I
guess that's why she didn't take me to the Vet. Well of
course, the Vet does cost money!

Louisa comes up with this idea! Their
friend, who is an old man, must be lonely, he has no
women in his life (Lucky Guy) and he has a kind face.

We will offer to give the bird to him as long as
he promises never to give it away. We will make him
feel as if he is really getting a gift from the charming and
quite pretty Louisa. --- He will go for it!

31

Well, he did, and this old geezer took me to his house in a horrible noisy car, scared me half to death.

You know, you have to look for the good side; he was living in a nice place that overlooked the Rio.

CHAPTER lll RE-ADOPTED

Let me explain, the Rio is a river that only runs in the rainy season and just a trickle or nothing the rest of the year. There are however lots of bugs and lots of birds.

This Old Guy whose name was Miguel had a nice Lanai or Veranda that was almost safe for a grounded bird.

Now the trouble was that the Lanai was tiled, with nice big red earth colored tile and it looked good. Miguel was only renting the place. You see he had a really mean and nasty landlady who was already making him pay for rebuilding the place. If we screwed up the Lanai it would cost heaps.

33

When I first looked at the place I thought;

Huh! I will have that floor a nice textured white in no

time. That apparently was not to be. Twice a day and

more often, if it was really hot, or I had been very busy,

Miguel would have to put on his thongs and come out

with a hose and a brush.

Miguel tried hard to be my friend.

He caught bugs for me. Went to a library and found

out what tribe I came from and what they ate. I was not

very nice to him though. I actually missed all the love

and petting. If he came near me I would peck him hard.

Then he would not try to pick me up. At night he built a

sort of cage around me with "Chicken Wire" so no cats

or owls could get to me I did not like it. It made me feel

like a dumb chicken. I was still very weak so I put up

with it.

On the third day I guess he felt I had settled in. He came and caught me with a towel and put me in the "Laundry Hamper". I was not too choosy about that. Then it got worse, he put me in the car and drove us down the highway. Huge big roaring trucks coming at us faster than a diving hawk. Wow!, I thought life as a bird was tough but really!. You humans must have nerves of steel.

He starts talking to me as if I could understand him which fortunately I could. He kept repeating himself though, as if he was talking to a baby or a chicken or something. That was very irritating.

"Yes Frankie we are going to the Vet. You should not be scared and try to stand still. We might hurt you a bit trying to straighten out your wing. We have to do that to fix it. Etc etc".

I really surprise Miguel when he takes me out of the car; I just stand motionless in the hamper while he carries me down the street and into the Vets examining room.

The Vet is the one who is nervous. He keeps saying "I do not usually treat Wild Animals". He is running around putting away anything that is fragile.

Miguel picks me up and sets me on the examining table. I stand there looking around but not moving my head. I guess I look a bit like a stuffed bird with loose wriggly eyes.

It had the desired effect the Vet stops what he is doing and stares at me. In a scared voice he asks "Is it all right?" (It! -- Huh! some manners!) With that I turn my head around and started preening my back feathers. Well you would have thought I had just spoken English   The Vet and his girl helper walk around and stare at me. The helper even tries to pet me. A good sharp peck on the end of her finger makes her jump back, and cures that idea. I go back to preening while the vet and Miguel discuss me.

"It is as if she knows we are trying to help her." the Vet says.

Miguel says "I think she does. She does not like it too much but she puts up with us."

The Vet is a good man he puts on cotton gloves and handles me slowly and gently. He lays me on my back and, with Miguel helping, spreads my wings out and flexes them. That hurts me. When it really hurts I squawk and kick and they stop.

In the end they decide on a plaster cast on what was left of the two bones of my arm, from what you would call my wrist to my elbow. Then when I am standing up again they put a red elastic bandage that wraps around my hand or wing tip and holds it up against the plaster cast.

After a while I can see the advantage, with my wing held up like that, I can walk again.

When I reach home and I am out and on to the Lanai I wait until Miguel leaves. Then I check it out; I can walk slowly, not quite run and I can jump or hop.

The jumping is the hardest as I have to learn to keep my feet together so as not to catch my bad wing. Not like the usual splayed leg landing stance of a carrier aircraft (copied from Gulls). Of course Miguel has been sneaky and is watching and clapping his hands and dancing around. It is very embarrassing, the man has no couth.   We both have a lot to learn from each other, and I began to realize that humans think birds are stupid.   The second morning that I was in the house he is amazed to see me standing in front of the Refrigerator staring at the Freezer. Well, it is breakfast time. I was here, I saw where the food came from yesterday. What does he thinkI am.

I wanted to say –Look your blessed Laptop does everything better and faster than those huge Desktops you used to have and they already know how to make a Laptop the size of a can of Sardines. My brain being small means nothing, just nothing!

CHAPTER IV   CRIPPLE

Photo of Frankie with Cast on wing.

The Cast and bandage does help quite a lot. I am

learning to walk around with it. I do not keep tripping

and falling as I used to.

43

Before I had the cast and stuff I would get so frustrated because I could not even jump up on a little brick. Half the times I tried I would keep falling down. I would struggle and usually end up on my back. When I was on my back I was totally helpless and could only wait for Miguel to come and help me, or someone to eat me.   Of course I figure it is his entire fault. Then I get so mad at the world. I wait until he has me right side up and is just setting me down and then I kick and peck him. Sometimes I overdo it and fall right back down on my back.   When I am in this undignified posture he squats down on his haunches and just laughs at me. I call him every bad name a bird ever had. He does not have to understand bird talk to get the message.

So this big human just squats there until I quiet down. I learn that if I peck him hard the second time he will just set me back down upside down on my BACK. Oh, I wish I could whack him with my wing. If only he was just my size.

My wing starts to heal and becomes really itchy under the cast and bandage. My large friend thinks he knows best as to when the cast should come off. The poor fool he has never ever even had a wing.

When I go to work at tearing off the cast he sneaks up grabs me and wraps me all up in an Ace Elastic Bandage. I look like one of those Egyptian Mummies with a bird's head, legs and feet. He laughs and laughs as I strut around cursing at him. In the end I

45

just gave up and left the Cast alone. I could not stand the laughter.

I guess he noticed that I always ran off and took a bath after he handled me. Anyway, he started keeping an old T-shirt handy to pick me up with. The food improves as well. Miguel knows a neat Fisherman named Martin who saves small Sardines and freezes them for me I can normally eat five or six Sardines, about eight to ten centimeters long, per day. The first time Martin came with the little fish they were fresh, some still wiggled. I went crazy I must have choked down ten at one sitting. It made me a very funny shape I could not quite close my beak. I found a nice shady spot and had a nice long siesta.

The funny thing about Mexico is that all
creatures seem to knock off about one o'clock and have a
Siesta. I felt safe as all the other animals were sleeping
too.

Miguel got a bee in his bonnet about me
getting fit. I thought it might be something to do with
flying again when my wing was healed.

The first lesson was to encourage me to Hop.
So he would hop in front of me, a couple of times. Then
when I eventually did the same he would reward me with
a Sardine. In the end, I could hop really high two or
three times without falling. When I got bored with
hoping lessons I stopped taking the sardines. Besides,
add two or three Sardines to my weight and the hopping

47

become difficult.

Miguel took to having me follow him around so he could show me things; where some juicy baby frogs lived, where a great big cockroach lived, and a bunch of other goodies. We actually became friends and if he was in the house I would want to be in there with him. That was a problem. The village was limiting water consumption by shutting it off for hours and finally for days.

You see, my bathroom habits are "very natural". When a girl has to go she goes, with a short back ward step and quick stop so it doesn't dirty the feathers.

Miguel was forever running around with water and a mop. My calling cards are quite corrosive. So when water is scarce ,he limits my time in the house That! does not suite me one bit.

Photo of The bird having bath.

Yeah ! I know what you guys are thinking . I know what you humans do with the Chickens and Turkeys you put in Pyrex roasting pans . Sick Sick Sick ! Realy -- eating Birds.!

CHAPTER V   Miniature Ostrich

We went back to the Vet twice and the third time he took the cast off. I still had to have a bandage on part time because my muscles were not very strong.

With no bandage I looked like a bird again.

When we reached home and Miguel had gone inside I tried flapping my wings just a little.

Oh, it hurt and I could not move my wings at all. Miguel heard me wimper, came out and sat down looking very sad and said "We have to talk":

The Vet and I do not know how to fix your bones so they are like new and we don't know where to attach all the tendons even if we could fix the bones.

51

Oh! My Wing I Just can't Look!

"Frankie there is no way that you are ever going to fly

again". Your little hollow bones were crushed and the

tendons broken   We can, with luck, get to the point

where you can move the inner wing enough that you will

not get stuck . You can run and hop but Fly --NEVER!

52

I Squawked at him and walked away.

I was depressed for a few days after that. I tried flapping my wings a number of times and   eventually gave it up. Wow! I guess he was right I was a miniature Ostrich

Miguel could tell what I was going thru and brought me pictures of Emus and Ostriches and all the flightless birds he could think of (most of them are extinct --that tells you something.) He even took me to meet a Parrot that had clipped wings. The wise guy laughed at me in human talk.

A million things went thru my mind but there was always a snag. I didn't have enough legs or arms to learn kick boxing. Maybe I could balance on my tail like a kangaroo and kick? No my legs were not long enough. I could put a knife on my beak. But I still had to eat with it. Oh, I don't know! The next program was being taken out to the veranda when he was eating his breakfast. He would lift me up on the table so I could see all the other birds that lived along the Rio.

There were ducks, a couple of Turkeys, Ibis and Hero and Parakeets and Cow birds and of course a couple of roosters and a lot of chickens.   Cows would come walking down the dry river bed with some men on horseback and a few dogs. Well, one day a dog went after a chicken, and that chicken took off running faster than the dog, at least until she reached the hen house. That Dog knew better than go near the hen house. That guy had a shotgun.

That afternoon when Miguel was having his siesta I picked out a track around the Palapa and ran and ran and ran. I did this for about two weeks.

He caught me at it and laughed at me.

"Oh so, Frankie you think you are going to be a chicken do you." Sweetheart, with those little short legs going at supersonic speed you are not going to beat a dog. The crabs yes and, "Keep it Up" Keep it up you never know -----there   are   a lot of Chihuahuas around here.   Talk about insulting!   The next step he took was to see if he could train me to roost in trees or something up high. He built little narrow walkways and put sardines at the end. I just squawked at him. He had not thought it through. Birds that roost in trees can all fly a bit so they do not fall out of the tree into the dog's mouth, and the other thing is they can wrap their toes right around a branch. My feet are made for walking on soft mud and swimming with. Silly Man!

56

I have this great phobia about being shut in, and hard as I try, I can not get rid of it. When Miguel built a nice secure enclosure for the night, out of chicken wire, I would try to live with it but it was no use. In a few hours I would be like "one possessed" pecking and pulling at the wire until even I became scared that I would break my beak. It was a major problem.

Miguel made a kind of maze with a spiral entrance out of Chicken wire. I slept in that for a few nights. Then one day we came out of the house and found the neighbor's cat eating my leftovers inside my "Secure Cage".

We had by working together sorted out how I could get in and out of the main house. There were four long steps and an iron and glass door that was usually open. When I first tried to get in the first step was too high for me to hop on to. The second step was too high one end but not as bad at the other end. So Miguel found a couple of nice flat bricks and put one leading up to the first step and the other at the other end of the second step.

I thought, "I had better play dumb", and then I can sneak into the house when I am not meant to be there. No go! He picks me up and puts me on the first brick. I stop and look at him and I could tell he was just going to keep handling me.

So I hopped up on the step ran down to the second brick, up the third step. Ran to the middle where it was lowest and hopped up and I was in the house and out to the bath on the veranda before he could say Jack Sprat.

He just stood there like a fool, then said "Smart little B---- aren't you."   Later on he was telling Garlic Breath and the "Girl with Few Clothes" "I bet it would take all day to teach a dog to do that".

CHAPTER Vl   THE PHOBIA

This feeling I had was a real problem. There were a lot of animals out there that looked at me and said "Ha Snack!" We had fortified the back yard and Veranda but some animals are almost impossible to keep out.   I understood the problem but I could not help it. Now that I felt healthy I just could not stand being caged. Miguel would come running out of his bed without his feathers several times a night if he heard a strange noise. He would shine his big flashlight around but never fast enough. He did startle a big Owl that I think was eyeing me but that was all. I am not sure if the light frightened the Owl or the sight of the man with no feathers on. It was scary!

We, that is, Miguel and I, did work out some games to play. When things were dull I would suddenly rush into the room where he was sitting and run around him as fast as I could. He responded by chasing me. Of course I could easily out whit him because I could run under tables and chairs and he would have to stumble around them. When I had given him a good workout I ended up conveniently standing looking at the Freezer, snack time?

We also had the butterfly hunt. In that part of the world on certain days there would be swarms of butterflies so we would leave the front door and the bedroom windows open and close the sliding screen doors to the veranda. Butterflies are not too smart so they end up trying to get out through the screen. I could walk along the bottom and eat the ones that were low down. Miguel gets a rolled up newspaper or egg lifter and bats the ones down from higher up and I jump up and catch them. Some are really tasty but I knew not to eat the black ones with red legs. He would get quite upset with me when after he had gone to particular effort to bat down a big black one I take one peck, see the red legs, drop it and walk away.

I had eaten about a hundred. After a while he started to learn. I like butterflies, dragon flies, small moths, but not big ones and I go mad about grasshoppers; cockroaches and small frogs. Spiders and Ants are not on my menu though.

The other thing I had to teach him was not to eat old fish. Fresh Sardine is wonderful. A two day old even if refrigerated is not acceptable. I mean if he had taken the trouble to carefully smell them he could have figured that out himself.

We Franklin People do not have molars, or any teeth for that matter, to grind up all our food, and pull corks out, open plastic bags and other things. So to compensate we are equipped with strong digestive juices. I can swallow large things like Fish Tails because they get dissolved on the way down so that even if they do not fit at first they will in a few minutes.

One day Miguel was killing himself laughing at me. I had snatched a good sized baby tuna tail out of his hand when he was about to cut it up. Well, it tasted good and I got the body part down my throat and the two fins were sticking out one each side of my mouth.

He said I looked like I had three beaks and chased me around to try and get it back. He was sure that I was going to choke on it. It all slid down nicely after three or four minutes.

There were a lot of different animals hanging around and I don't think Miguel knew about most of them he always made so much noise that they had lots of time to hide. If I left any food in my dish at night I had a procession. First the land crabs would come and try and grab it. Then Rat that lived under the house had a run at it.

Then the neighborhood flea hostel (a dog), or one of the neighborhood cats would come sniffing around the gate.

I would be pacing up and down outside the front door, wanting to come into the house. I would even peck at the glass to get his attention. It was no use by the time he got up from his reading and scraped the chair across the floor, a whole Noah's Ark of animals could have run away. So there he would stand looking at me and I am sure he was thinking: So what's new, you just want to con me into letting you in so you can poop on the floor some more. So forget it already! Get back in your run and be safe and secure. A minute and a half before I had been chased out of my "Secure Run" by a land crab that outweighed me. It is so hard to communicate with Humans they always mistrust you and think the worst and just cannot first stop and consider all the possibilities.

Miguel was deaf as a door nail and could not see without his glasses so he was some protector. ! I, on the other hand, had all my senses but could not control my emotions.

I could not even endure it for long in the main house with all the screens and doors closed. How was he going to build a secure roosting place for me?

What I needed was a marsh, or a tidal island, or sand bank, and even then I needed wings.

He talked to me about using drugs, some sort of tranquilizer so I would stay in a cage overnight. The problem is how much Valium he should give to a six ounce (180gram) bird when an 80Kg human only needed one tiny pill.

We, Miguel and I, would have other outings though. We would drive down to the beach. I guess he thought that it would be fun for me to run on the beach and try and catch little crabs and other goodies. The funny thing was I found it kind of scary.

There were a lot of big Gulls and Frigate birds and Vultures and they all looked at me, as if I was the next meal. Then of course there were the dogs as well. We tried it a couple of times at different hours but I would always start edging back to the car and the palm trees after about five minutes. I think Miguel was a little disappointed. Now, if he had just taken me somewhere where there were Sardines it might have been different.

69

I suppose that if you come from a family like mine it can be difficult. I grew up like my predecessors for the last 100,000 years living in the open.

We are a successful tribe because we fly away from predators. We have no Burrow, Cave, or House to hide in, we just fly.

We Franklins prefer two types of food, Grasshoppers, (Locusts if you like) and small fish. Where there are lots of Franklins you do not have to worry about Plagues of Locusts because we eat them when they are young. The female hopper digs a little trench in late summer in which to lay her eggs.

She covers the eggs with a type of foam (to prevent Mildew) and fills in the trench. In the early spring as the ground thaws, the young Hoppers come out of the ground. Right at that time a lot of very hungry Franklins arrive having just flown all the way from Chile or sometimes even further.

The early Mormons gave thanks to God for saving them from starvation due to a plague of Hoppers. It was Franklins who saved them. They were the ones who arrived just then and ate the Hoppers.

Miguel came out one day with a magazine that he said he bought at the airport. He read me a bunch of it, some of which I understood. It was some kind of report about the prairie farmers in Alberta and Saskatchewan around where we nest. How when they drain all the little lakes and sloughs and plant more wheat all they get is more grasshoppers, and less wheat!

I don't know? Lets see now!—Less lakes = Less Franklins= More Grasshoppers = Less Wheat. Hmm, that's pretty straightforward for a Gull .   I guess you human minds must work differently. Oh Well!!

The Summer time was upon us and I was feeling quite healthy. I started to get these nesting feelings I took to gathering long stalks of dead grass and some light sticks in one end of the Lanai. I think Miguel thought I had gone mad at first, but he figured it out eventually. We Franklin's build our nests in the shallow water reeds and grasses on the edges of lakes and sloughs in the prairies. We quite often congregate in big colonies of twenty to fifty thousand.

The Nests are just a pile of dead long grass .and rushes woven in amongst the grasses and reeds growing in the shallow water. The nest gets waterlogged and slowly sinks all season. We have to keep putting more stuff on it. It works well because heavy animals can't walk on the nests or they sink. The bigger animals have to wade or swim to get to the eggs or chicks and then the whole colony of birds will give them a bad time.

I kept watch for any Franklin Gulls that might fly over but I only saw them once. There were three of them and they were high up in the sky. I called and called but they did not hear. Miguel came out to see what all the racket was about. Of course he could see nothing. So he went inside and fetched the binoculars and was then quite amazed. "Frankie they do look like Franklin's. Wow, you really have good eyes they must be at two or three thousand feet." pretty much gave up after that. I mean what right minded Gull is going to want to mate with a gull that can't even fly. I stopped gathering nesting materials except for one piece to remind me of normal life.

In the Colony there are single or one year old birds that do not have a nest. They will sometimes adopt a couple and help them build or keep up their nest. And sometimes they even help incubate the eggs.

There was an iron gate that the man had covered with chicken wire that led from the Back Yard to the dirt road. I was getting so feisty that I took to attacking that gate at times.

Miguel opened it up one day and told me "So you think you are ready for the world, do you, Frankie". Good, lets the two of us walk up the road and visit

Neighbor Paul. Miguel walked out slowly, calling to me all the time. I started to follow him. It was OK at first.

I chased a butterfly and then a small lizard. We had walked about twenty meters up the street when up by the highway half a kilometer away this big red gravel truck turned in to our road. It was making that Pop Pop Pop Pop, such a noise it frightened me. I ran back thru the gate as fast as any chicken ever could. When Miguel followed, laughing, he could not find me. I was hiding under an Elephant Ear leaf. I never went out that gate again.

So my world was now the back yard and the Lanai, when I could get out there. Boy, some step down for a bird that could fly to South Africa when she had two good wings.

We Franklins get around a lot there are records of sightings and photos from Israel, England and Norway and South Africa even Western Australia and China. Miguel showed me a map he downloaded one day. I knew about most of that because we know how to find our way back to the Prairies to nest each year. We don't need a map. It's the only place we nest.

Most of us spend Northern Winter down on the west coast   in places called Uruguay and Chile where there are lots of small fish, my favorite Sardines.

My Name Is Frankie
Michael A Pope

CHAPTER VII

The Rains Came

Summer was getting on and the rainy season started. When it finally does rain in that part of Mexico it really rains. First the thunder and lightning in the early night. Then after all the warning, here it comes. You cannot hear yourself think for the racket. The rain pours down. The Thunder crashes. The lightning is so bright it makes everything look white.

The Rio floods from nothing to a meter deep in two nights.

The road becomes a river. I was scared the whole house was going to sail down it.

I like standing in an open spot when it first starts raining. Miguel says it looks as if I am trying to catch rain drops. I am not. I just like the feeling of those big cold drops landing on me it sooths me and makes me remember when I was free. When I was a whole bird person and could come and go as I wanted.

This weather did not help my Phobia I was even less secure. I could not hear anything creeping up on me. I could not even see right after a lightning flash. I was helpless. I tried to stay in the shelter under the plastic table, it was Claustrophobic, and the rain beating on the plastic was too much.

Well the Miguel was worried about me, he even put together a shelter on the Lanai but it was flooded in no time. The drains could not keep up, it was ten centimeters deep. The wind really swooped down there too. I took one look and turned back into the house.

So the next night we tried leaving the Lanai screen door open a bit. I would sleep in the house. That was a no go there was a big Iguana that was taking shelter. He maybe a herbivore but did not look very friendly to me. I fled to the Lanai and nearly drowned out there.

Then we had a week's respite the river went back down to a foot or so deep. You could walk up the road, just. Lots of new birds came to look for food in the receding river. I was able to stand up on the lanai table and swear at all of them. They all heard and noticed but looked away.

The next storm we had was a bad one.

We put some Palm tree branches on top of the plastic table in the back yard to kill the noise and built a clever spiral entrance.

He forced me into it at nightfall and sat with his evening Gin and watched me for an hour more. Just to make sure that I did not try and get out.

The storm arrived later in the night. I saw him in a lightning flash sitting back from the glass door where he thought I could not see him checking on me.

I was out in the middle of the yard in as clear a space as I could find. I was a fearless Franklin's Gull. No hiding in burrows or caves for me.

Miguel went back to bed. I must have dozed off. I had been day dreaming, thinking about the day of the 'Accident" nearly five months earlier that had got me into this mess.

I guess I should tell you. It was greed that was my downfall. I was cruising down the surf line at first light looking for breakfast. The sea was calm no wind at all. I had not seen any fish and I was hungry. It was past my breakfast time. I had been blown north from Tehuantepec by a tropical storm that was strong for about a week. I had lost my Franklin family; I had been too greedy hunting Sardines. Suddenly out of the corner of my eye I saw them a ball of sardines being attacked by some big fish from below I did not stop to think, or look around I just dove straight for them.

I got a Sardine but just then a big old Pelican's beak hit me in the wing driving me into the water and Oh!--pain as my bones broke. I could have drowned if old Mr. Pelican had not fished me out and set me on the surface.

The Pelican was very kind about it he had started his dive a lot higher up and was going straight down at full speed when I swooped between him and the water. There was nothing he could do. He was quite upset ..   He had to just leave me there outside the breakers and fly off to rejoin his family

So here I am dreaming away in the middle of a war zone with the thunder and the lightning. It is cold and windy and my feathers are getting all ruffled.

85

It is good, I thought, that Louisa came along that day and saved me. If I had drowned I would have died just a free ignorant bird. Now I know Louisa and Miguel and the Vet and all those human people who are my friends. I wonder how many other birds there are who have human people friends? Not counting Parrots they are just sluts

Not many I bet. Especially Gulls we are too independent.

How about the humans? Have I taught them anything? Miguel knows not to eat butterflies with red legs. He can tell now when fish is really fresh-- without asking me! . Do you think the others are learning anything? I think I would have to live to be an awfully old Gull before Miguel could understand everything I said especially with his being deaf and half blind. He understands more though! Wouldn't that be great if I could talk to him? We could write a book together! Sometimes when I start to day dream I sort of drift away from reality. Kind of like, when you find a big hot thermal over the Prairies aaaaand you just keep circling. Going up and up with no effort.-------- The fields and lakes get smaller and

smaller and it is so peaceful so beautiful----.

I got up in the morning went out as usual to say good morning to Frankie and listen to her usual demands for immediate Sardines.   But she was not there.

There was a lot of trash that had blown here and there in the wind and rain and a lot of blood red Bougainvillea flowers that had blown down but no Frankie. I searched and searched and eventually found a few feathers and three or four drops of blood no sign of my friend.

I went and got a cup of coffee and sat and looked around the empty garden. It suddenly seemed awfully quiet and lonely.

I eventually found a skull and beak and some feathers outside an Opossum's hole under the house. They usualy kill chickens by sneeking up and biting their heads off ---so at least it was quick and painless.

One day, I hope we will learn all that the birds know.

ADDENDUM---- ABOUT FRANKLIN'S GULLS

Franklin's gulls, Bonaparte's Gulls, and Sabine's Gulls, are three of the species of gulls whose behavior and life are quite different from the larger garbage dump frequenting Gulls species that we see more of.

Franklin's nest on the edges of sloughs and shallow lakes in the Prairies.

Bonaparte's nest in the Coniferous forests surrounding Northern Lakes

The Sabine nests on the Arctic shoreline. These three species do not frequent garbage dumps

All three species eat principally small and large insects and aquatic crustaceans, invertebrates and small fish.

91

The Franklin's are unique in that they molt twice a year presumably to offset the wear and tear on their flight feathers from their migration from the Prairies to Chile and back each year.

The Franklin's route takes them south thru the central plains across Texas to the Gulf of Mexico. They appear to follow the coast of Mexico to Tehuantepec where they cross over to the pacific shore before proceeding down the coast of South America.

The upwelling from the Humboldt Current along the west coast of South America provides nutrition for large schools of Sardines, Pilchards and other small fish. El Nino Effects shift the emphasis of the current north and south year by year and the birds follow.

The Franklin's familiar black helmet and mask becomes less pronounced in the winter. The Rosy hue to their chest feathers and the red tip of the beak are their mating colors and are not evident at all in the "northern winter plumage".

The life span of these birds appears to be about nine years. They all return to the north every year mating in their second or third summer and producing two or three eggs. The male and female share the nest building and incubation and are apparently monogamous at least for one year.

These gulls are very gregarious forming nesting colonies of twenty to fifty thousand individuals.

There are records of whole colonies totally abandoning nesting sites if they are molested repeatedly. This makes the species vulnerable to human encroachment.

The eggs hatch in twenty to twenty three days and the young birds are swimming within days and flying in less than a month.

Franklins are very efficient fliers and extremely maneuverable. They can feed on small insects in flight in the same way that Swallows or Martins do.

Initialy I thought that The gulls just liked soaring way up high in those sunnyday Thermals. Then a Glider pilot freind of mine straightened me out. There are lot of bugs in a field or hedge row and many of them fly well with a good rate of climb but the fatter ones and some of the lighter ones do not have a good diving speed and they get caught in the thermals. They can fly up till they get to thin air and their wing loading gets too high but they cannot get out of the up-draft. So the Franklin Gulls wait for them and solve their problem. Measurements' indicate they can fly long distances at thirty five miles an hour. This relatively high speed and their ability to swim and feed on the ocean surface explain why they are sighted nearly all over the world. Groups of birds are observed making their way north on the West Coast of Africa apparently heading back to the Prairies. There are sightings all the way from Hong Cong to Perth in Western Australia ,to Israel in the eastern Mediteranian   One hypothesis for the distinctive summer – winter plumage change is that the summer plumage is an indication of sexual maturity and ability to mate.

HYPOTHESIS -- HOWMANY HOWMANY FRANKLINS

To be fair to the biologists involved it is really hard to count Franklin Gulls they do not always nest in the same places and the sometimes shift homes and they are not tolerant of disturbances.   From what I read there seems to be agreement that the population was diminishing at about three point nine percent from 1966 onwards until 2012 . That would work out to us having less than 20% of what we had in sisty six.   We have no data before 66 but we know there were huge flocks that frightened he Farmerswhen the white man first started farming wheat in the 1800s   If Alberta Province has it right at about one point three million breeding pairs in that Province now . Then we could easily have had six times as many before the white man.   Or perhaps a North American population of ten to twenty million pairs or more.

This year Alberta Government is offering to pay the farmers $ 4.00 /Acre to spray for Hopper's

(Grass hoppers) The farmer's cost averages $12.00 an acre for spraying. Last year Alberta had 400,000 acres in "Winter Wheat" alone and the government will spray this year they claim two and a half million acres total including roadways and access. I am sure the reader knows this also wipes out innumerable creatures that are really helpful such as bees and many more species. The Franklin appear to represent Natures natural balance for Plagues of Locusts (Hoppers they are called today --less threatening --Political Speak) Maybe this is yet another illustration of "Do not screw with Nature and drain lakes" Kill all the beavers and take out their Dams.

The Gulls certainly add a lot of high Nightrogen Fertilizer with their feces which is expensive too (up to $75.00 /acre for some farmers)

. But then Bird's and Beavers do not vote and support political parties and fertilizer and spray companies do--- Lavishly!

Thanks for reading ===== I am not sure what we should do. Maybe just read more!   Maybe just impose   hateful government limits on what people and companies can do to the land scape. Obviously owners are not smart enough!   Oh Well   You should not expect too much of us ---- We cannot even Fly!

www.ingramcontent.com/pod-product-compliance
Lightning Source LLC
Chambersburg PA
CBHW070750290526
45795CB00002B/544